The book you have in your hand is transcribed from an interview that was recorded in August 2014.

Doug Alexander, the founder of Triple Win Inc. and the creator of the GPS Process, discusses the failure of traditional Financial Planning in dealing with the most important and fundamental issue for Canadians in the Middle Class.

"How do I afford my life!"

Doug explains that he developed the GPS Process to deal with the affordability gap that he saw in his own life and how his solution has revolutionized the lives of hundreds of his clients.

The interview shows the experience, thoroughness, creativity and passion behind this truly revolutionary financial process.

Here's What's Inside

5 **Introduction**

7 **The Better Life...Paid in Full!**

9 **Chapter 1 – The Problem**

15 **Chapter 2 – The Magnitude of the Problem**

16 **Chapter 3 – The Conventional Approach**

20 **Chapter 4 – The Solution**

44 **Chapter 5 – Next Steps**

46 **Appendix**

48 **About the Author**

The Better Life… Paid in Full

Take all the Hopes, Dreams and Wishes you have for your family. Lay them all out on a table in front of you. Now write, "PAID IN FULL" across all of them. That's the starting point for your Better Life.

By Doug Alexander

Copyright © 2014 Doug Alexander
All rights reserved.
ISBN-10: 1502930390
ISBN-13: 978-1502930392

Introduction

The Better Life...Paid in Full!

Ontario, Canada
October 2014

Having a passion for math, I've always looked at life a little differently than most. Forty years ago I sat down with pen and paper in hand and extrapolated out my financial future from my early 20's through my retirement years. What I  found from that process was that the conventional method being taught to us was fundamentally flawed.

No matter how I tweaked the numbers (saving more, earning more, higher gains) there was no realistic plan when using the conventional methods. Nothing I found could make up for the fact that our generation was going to live a lot longer. We either had to plan to work into our 80s, which just isn't what I wanted for my family and me or we were going to have to find a better way.

This book is a result of my frustration at seeing into the future so long ago and realizing before I even started that the system was doomed for failure. In the story that follows, I share what we found to be the only viable long-term solution for middle class Canadians to live their Better Life today and tomorrow. In the book, I walk you through what has been proven to work with hundreds of our clients to ensure their future of living The Better Life.

I hope this book educates you and helps change your way of thinking about your approach to your life and encourages you to find the better way.

Enjoy the book!

To your Better Life!

Doug Alexander

CPA, CMA

The Better Life...Paid in Full!

Susan: Good afternoon, this is Susan Austin and I'm excited to be here today, interviewing Doug Alexander. Doug is going to be sharing with us his thoughts and ideas on how we can live a Better Life both now and in our future years. Welcome Doug.

(The following is the transcript of this interview)

Doug: Thank you very much Susan. Glad to be here.

Susan: Great. Why did you want to write a book on The Better Life?

Doug: For the Baby Boomers the cast is set. For most of them, their only choice for achieving a Better Life is to continue working because most of them haven't saved enough in their working years to be able to retire and live comfortably. For Gen X and Gen Y, there's still time for them to really do something that's transformational. They can not only live The Better Life while they're in the working years, but they can also save so they can continue to have The Better Life in their retirement years. The definition of The Better Life is going to become more complete and meaningful and have a lot more substance for the Gen X and Gen Y than for the Baby Boom generation, which I am part of.

What triggered me to write this book is that we have had discussions with many individuals in the 35 - 50 age group. This is our ideal client group. It is very clear that there is a financial gap that exists for these individuals. A gap that only gets bigger if they follow the conventional methods. I'm excited about using this book as a method to get the message across in a much broader way than we have in the past.

Susan: We don't really get this information on how to live The Better Life in college nor anywhere else for that matter, do we?

Doug: No, we don't. Colleges teach you best practices. However, best practices only get you to the conventional way to spend and save for your future. To really move society forward you have to go beyond best practices. The ideas that I'm going to be sharing with you today are based on those same principles, but we've taken it far beyond that.

Susan: Well, I'm excited to hear what you have to share with us today.

Chapter 1 – The Problem

Doug: A major challenge arises during the working years of your life. How do you allocate your resources? Can I afford to live a Better Life today and still save enough money along the way so that I can continue living that Better Life throughout retirement? One of the things the conventional method states is, "I have to sacrifice today for my future." We want to change that paradigm. You do not have to sacrifice today. You can live The Better Life today and be able to continue to do so in your retirement years when you have even more choices and more selection.

There are two phases in your life after you finish school. These are the working years and the retirement years. We're going to talk about how those years get allocated. It's clear that the conventional method of financial planning didn't work for the Baby Boomers. We are seeing that, for the most part, Baby Boomers aren't able to retire when they wanted to and how they wanted to.

Everyone is familiar with the concept "Freedom 55" which was a program that said we could retire at age 55. It was a great marketing concept. The problem was it didn't have any substance behind it from a mathematical perspective or even from a life perspective. With the clear proof that the process doesn't work, you would think that conventional thinking would be looking at making things better. But things haven't improved much from when I first looked at this. When my wife and I got engaged, I sat down and took a look at our life into the future. That was when I was in my mid 20's. I laid out a plan. Keep in mind, in those days, the mid 70's; it was all done by pen and paper. There were no PC's like we have today. What I discovered was, "we couldn't afford our life!"

My background is accounting, finance and economics. My wife's background is IT, so we had a very good future ahead of us. We were going to earn very good incomes, but even taking all that into account I realized we couldn't afford our lives. I made two major assumptions in our plan that turned out to be totally incorrect. First, I had assumed we would never pay more than $100,000 for a house. Back in the mid 70's you could get a nice house for about $80,000. Secondly, I assumed we were only going to have two children. We ended up having four. Had I layered those two assumptions into our plan correctly, the gap would have been even bigger.

As a result of this gap, I knew I needed a solution, so I went out in search of people who I thought would have the solution we needed. I went out and found investment advice, insurance advice, tax advice and legal advice. But I found nobody pulling it together into a cohesive plan. I then started on a journey that has taken me to where I am today. When I showed these experts my analysis, which was about 40 or 50 pages long, most of them had no idea about the math and most of them didn't think it was a problem because they were working with high net worth clients which of course, in those days I wasn't. We went in search of a solution and what we're going to share with you in the book today is the results of that search.

The principles haven't changed from 35 - 40 years ago. However, with the tools that are available today we do it a lot more efficiently and we do it on a more expanded basis.

Back when I was in my mid 20's we had the same goals that a Gen X-er or a Gen Y has in their 20's. Those goals haven't changed. In the past 40 years there hasn't been much advancement in the financial services being offered. There are a lot of products out there, but nothing that pulls it all together for the middle class Canadian wanting to live a Better Life.

Susan: You said you couldn't afford your life Doug. What do you mean by that?

Doug: I started adding up what our life was going to cost. I took a look at our annual living expenses, which included the costs of operating a house, operating a car, food, vacations, medical expenses, etc. Then I thought about our future and what commitments we would have to pay for. Things like buying and paying for a house, all the cars we were going to buy over our life and the maintenance they were going to need. Then I added in the impact of having children, becoming a one income family for a period of time, maternity leave, putting the kids through school and sports activities, paying for weddings, and post-secondary expenses.

When you take a look at that complete scope, most people don't realize that when you add up existing personal debt, your mortgage and future commitments, they can total more than $1 million dollars. I'm talking about in terms of today's dollars. This doesn't even include the day-to-day living expenses. People don't see the complete picture and the complete cost of living their life. When you take a look at your income you don't have a lot left over. They don't have extra money to save for their future.

One of the keys to our process is that we get people to look at the big picture and we actually add it all up. If I was to say to you, "Susan, over the next 25 years, how much are you going to spend on cars?" Most people aren't able to answer that. They'll say, "Oh, I'm not quite sure." So we take them through a process to get them to think about the cost of cars.

"How long do you normally keep your cars?"

  "Well, maybe I keep them for six years."

   "Are you a two-car family?"

   "Yes."

   "So, you're going to buy a car every three years. How much do you usually spend on your cars?"

   They'll say, "Oh, about $35,000."

That means over 24 years you're going to buy eight cars and at $35,000 each that's a quarter million plus inflation. That's about $350,000 you are going to be spending just on buying automobiles. This is always an eye opening experience. They tell me, "Wow, I didn't think I was going to spend that much on cars."

When we start adding in all the other pieces of life, they start to realize that "This is a much bigger number than we imagined."

At this point it all starts coming together.

"Where do I get the money to pay for all of it?"

"While I'm paying for all these commitments, how am I supposed to be saving so I can continue my Better Life in retirement?"

It's a question not enough people are asking.

It's really thinking things through and building the awareness and adding it all up. It's not difficult to do. Everybody knows how to add numbers up from a tactical perspective, but very few people know how to add them from a strategic perspective.

Susan: I don't know that I'd want to see that number because it would probably scare the heck out of me.

Doug: Yes and that's really what gets clients to stop and think about the total cost. Until they know the path they are headed down, things don't add up properly. They don't really want to deal with the reality of it. They're like an ostrich with its head in the sand. We say, "You don't have to ignore it, let's identify it. Let's scope it out and let's find out if there's technology there that can help you deal with your reality."

Susan: The Baby Boomers didn't save enough and the Gen X-ers are on that same course. A lot of people's solution is to suggest we just need to cut back and save more. You're suggesting something different?

Doug: I'm suggesting a combination. When you get into our process budgeting does play an important role, but we get people to budget in terms of a conversation. It is amazing what happens when you sit down and you ask people what they spend their money on and then you get the couple to talk about it,

"I spend so much on this," and you say, "What value do you get out of that?" Here's what I mean by value. You don't pay your property tax to get a house. You pay your property tax to get a home and in that home you have special events. You have birthday parties, anniversaries. You cry and you celebrate. That's what makes a house a home. However, if you don't pay your property tax you don't get to be in that home. If you don't pay your utilities you can't enjoy your home. If it's 35°C outside you go where it's cool or if its 0°C you go where it's warm. It's a home not a house.

It's amazing what happens when people start to look at their spending in terms of their life, their values and their emotions. Some of the best memories I have in my life are Christmas time with my family. I wouldn't trade that living room-dining room experience for anything. That's why I have a home. Yes, I have a house so it provides shelter, but I have a home so my kids can come over Sunday afternoon and spend a great afternoon with us. When you look at your money in terms of those things it becomes a conversation that's transformational. It's no longer a budget about property tax, heat and hydro. As part of our process we move the clients to the level of being engaged with it, not just playing budgeting. It is important to understand the "what" and "why" of how you spend your money.

Chapter 2 – The Magnitude of the Problem

Let's talk about the magnitude of the problem we are facing. If someone is 35 years of age, actuarially speaking, they have a very good chance of living to age 90. If that's the case, you could very well have your working years from ages 25 - 65 and your retirement years from 65 - 90. If you look at that and you reference back to what I said a while ago about your spending being $1 million or more, it doesn't take rocket science to figure out I'm going to spend the next 20 years or more paying these bills. In other words, paying for my day-to-day living, paying off my existing mortgage and paying for future commitments. At best I might have 10 years to save for retirement and we know that 10 years isn't enough time to save for 25 years of retirement. We have what I call a **"20 – 10 – 25" problem**. In summary 20 years of major spending, 10 years of saving, and 25 years of retirement. The numbers don't add up.

Let me give you an example. A person working for a company with a company pension plan, may start at age 25 and then work 30 years until age 55. A Pension Plan like this is what's called a "Defined Benefits Plan," which means that you take your number of years worked times a percent to get your pension income. A lot of employers in Canada have these. You're going to end up with an income that averages 60% of your best 5 years. With our years of experience, we have a lot of clients like this and we've found that the pension isn't enough for them despite contributing for 30 years into the plan.

See the Case Study for a full understanding of the magnitude of the problem- Appendix A

Chapter 3 – The Conventional Approach

So on your own you can only save for 10 years. Add to this that for most of Gen X and Gen Y the "Defined Benefits Pension Plan" is dying. The math is irrefutable. It doesn't take much to figure out that you are going to come up short. You can't save enough in 10 years to live for 25, which in essence is what has happened to the Baby Boomers. This is the big problem. By the time people get to their late 50's - early 60's, the fortunate ones may have company and government pension plans such as Canada Pension Plan and Old Age Security. At best they have no personal debt. You hear in the news right now about all these people retiring with personal debt. That's why a lot of Baby Boomers have to continue working.

If you want to have The Better Life continue in your retirement, you not only have to retire with no personal debt, you have to retire with a substantial net asset base.

To accomplish this takes a very different approach because the reality of life is you've got major commitments from age 35 - 55 and they have to be paid for. How do you pay for those commitments as well as having an asset base to continue the Better Life in your retirement years? The conventional approach as you can see simply doesn't work.

Susan: The numbers don't add up.

Doug: Yes. Let's review what the conventional approach to this problem is. If you were sitting in front of someone with the conventional approach and they were able to do the financial analysis to come up with these numbers, they would say one of three things to you. The conventional way would say, "Susan, you have to save more money," and likely that's not realistic. It won't result in your living The Better Life now because for that to work you have to spend less. The second thing they'll say is we have to figure some way to get greater growth in your investments, but certainly in the last 10 years the market has shown that isn't possible. Over the long-term getting 6% - 8% is probably realistic and probably closer to 6% than 8%. Then the third thing they'll suggest is you have to work longer. As I said, working longer is the solution the Baby Boomers are living with right now. The financial services industry has told the Baby Boomers they just need to work longer.

I was watching a TV show on CBC just recently about retirement in Canada and the failure of pension plans. The group of experts resoundingly said, "Well, there's really not much of a problem with Baby Boomers. They just have to work longer." Well, I'd like to give my clients greater choices than having to work longer. I'd like to give them greater choices than having to live on less. I'd like to give them greater choices so they are not depending upon the market to give them 10%, to 15% growth."

To achieve The Better Life now and later you need to find a better way of doing Financial Planning. It might turn out that the person has to save more money or work longer, but with the GPS Process they have to save a lot less money than they would with conventional methods. With our process they have to work a lot less as well.

Susan: Perfect. The conventional method says people should get to retirement by saving more money. But they are already tapped with all these life expenses.

Doug: The conventional method would take you through a budgeting exercise. It may even take you through a somewhat comprehensive planning model to help understand other aspects of your spending profile. They might include items and events like house upgrades, cars, kid's education, weddings and maybe getting a cottage. They may do all that, then when they run the numbers using their model they come away and tell you, "You're short," and then they'll say, "You have to cut back and put more money in or you will have to work longer."

Susan: Or you've got to get a bigger return on your money...

Doug: The interesting thing is the financial service industry is backing away from that response. They will say, "You know guys, when it really comes down to it, you're going to get 6% - 8% growth and we've run the model with that and there's still not enough." They pass the buck back to the client. One of my biggest irritants with the financial services industry is they're blaming the client for the problem and even though the client may be part of the problem, the financial services industry hasn't come up with innovative ideas for the middle-class Canadian. They're only interested in high net worth clients.

Let's be realistic. If you come to me with $1 million Susan, I can turn it into $2 million 10 years from now, no big deal. If you come to me with a negative net worth of $300,000 excluding your house, turning that into $1 million with all the commitments along the way is hard work. That needs an accelerator technology. The industry isn't addressing these folks because they're interested in high net worth clients.

Our ideal client is not a high net worth individual. It's your middle-class Canadian, Gen-X and Gen-Y who don't start off with $1 million. Getting higher growth isn't realistic and the industry has come to that conclusion. Putting more money in, to the tune of an extra $20,000, $30,000 or $40,000 per year to close the gap, is not realistic. These individuals are already managing their money reasonably well and there isn't any money left over at the end of the month. It's got to come from someplace else.

Susan: It's like the formula for success here is broken because we need so much more to live on now, and we live so much longer.

Doug: Yes, from day one the math doesn't add up. It just doesn't work and they're trying to make something that's broke, work. It's like taking the horse and buggy and saying, "We're going to feed the horse so it's better," and I'm over here saying, "Forget the horse and buggy, go to the car." I don't care if you have Secretariat as your horse. The horse and buggy is never going to go as fast as the car, so let's move to the car. The financial service industry continues to insist upon making the horse and buggy work better.

Susan: We walk around feeling guilty because we don't have enough saved up but you're saying the models broken.

Doug: That's exactly correct. There's guilt out there for sure. "You should be saving more," they say. I say, "Financial service industry, what value are you adding?"

Chapter 4 – The Solution

Most people don't realize they're working with a broken model. They're trying to get a broken model to work. It's not all bad. We are not saying that you throw the baby out with the bathwater. There's a lot of good content in the conventional model. What you have to do is move it to a whole new level. It's the process of adding to the model, not wiping it out and starting from scratch, because we don't have to start from scratch.

When the conventional methods are applied they just don't impact middle-class Canadian families. When the GPS Process is applied, it not only transforms individual families' lives, it can impact the whole economy. We realized that if we took the impact that we have on an individual middle-class Canadian family and we took it to a broader scale it would increase government revenues. It would allow us to help the government pay off the debt faster. It would bolster our economy and I'm now going to go back and contradict myself, it would result in greater stock market growth, which means you can get greater growth that would help solve the problem.

When this approach, which we're focusing on at the individual level, gets applied at the broader level, it transforms every component. It is that powerful. We have close to 400 clients and their economies have all been transformed with this process. The transformation is not just restricted to the Canadian individual. It could filter up and flow through to the government, to the economy and to the stock market.

Let's talk about what this concept is. If I make any statements and I can't deliver on them it's all for naught. To explain the concept let me give you an example. If you are a forestry company, when you cut down a tree you will re-plant two right away. It takes 30 plus years for a tree to grow to maturity so you can harvest it again. That example is one of the key basics of our process. You should harvest and plant at the same time. You don't harvest and then plant 20 years later because if you do, going back to our 20 - 10 - 25 model, you won't be able to start to harvest until 30 years after you've planted. In other words, you have to work until you're 85.

Ironically speaking, if you work the numbers it's not too far off with what most Baby Boomers are going to have to do. If they spent from age 35 – 55 paying for commitments, and they start to plant significantly at age 55, they would then only be able to harvest in their 80s because it just wouldn't have had a chance to grow. Since the conventional method looks at things sequentially, which separates spending and income, you cannot integrate the approach. In our process we do them at the same time and with the same dollar.

Our solution is called the "GPS Process". Most people know the GPS as a global positioning system. We call it, GOALS, PARTNERSHIPS AND STRATEGIES.

You begin to understand your goals as you discuss your Life Journey. It's important to ask people, "What's important to you about money?" We find that when we get people talking about their life they spend most of the time talking about their values not about money. Then based upon their values we can start building their plan. I'll say, "OK, if what's important to you is sending your kids to post secondary school, how much is that going to cost?" Do you see how the dollars flow out of their values? The dollars don't flow into the values. The dollars flow out of the values and that's a key difference. You are becoming engaged with your money.

Tactically you have to understand your existing financial position. The boring things like: "How much is my house worth? How much debt do I have in mortgage, car loans? Do I have any investments like RRSP's etc.?" Then we look at income and spending profile. If we sit down with someone who is 35, we look at the next 20 to 25 years of their life, from an income perspective. "What income do you have now?"

"How much do you see in the future?"

Are they eligible for pensions, whether or not they'd be company or government? What are they? The person begins to understand the complete scope over that 20-25 year period as to what their income is.

All of a sudden the numbers become relevant. We're talking about the vibrancy, the fiber, the importance of your life and the money, the numbers flow out of it.

From income we move to spending profile. We look at your day to day living expenses. This is really hard for many people because they have never really analyzed it. To help, we can get you to fill out how much you spend running your house, i.e. property tax, how much you spend on car, maintenance, gas, etc.

Sometimes I'll ask, "How many times do you fill the tank up each week?" and we multiply it out. We can look at all the activities in your life and the numbers that flow from them. In your house, what do you have to do? I take you on a virtual tour of your house, starting with your driveway. Is it in good repair? Will it have to be replaced? If so, when?

We'll repeat this with the living room, dining room, and the rest of your house. You start to visualize in your head, "I want to improve my kitchen. I want to do this. I want to do that." In other words it's part of your life. The numbers flow from your life.

It's the conversation that brings out all these wonderful elements of their life that are so important to capture from a planning perspective.

Then we take a look at their family.

"Do you have children, how many?"

"I have two kids."

"Well, you want to help them through school?"

"Absolutely! I think they're going to get married as well."

Whenever we think about children in this way it causes us to reflect and really engage with our lives. The activities flow out of your lives. We get them to talk about their lives and to actually live their life out in our conversation. I've had people sit down with me for 90 minutes and they live their life. Afterwards I'll ask them

"If that's the life you live is that your Better Life?"

I want to hear back "If I lived that life that would be fabulous."

If I don't, I say, "Well, what would make it fabulous?"

"But I don't know about you Susan, I want to live The Better Life. I want to live a fabulous life. I don't want to live a hum drum life."

On paper you can plan whatever you want, however, living it can be a different scenario. Some people may want to buy a cottage. Some people may want to buy a boat. Some want to travel extensively. We include those kinds of things in their plan. In other words, I hate to be a broken record, but the numbers flow from your life. They don't flow into it. They flow out of it.

The next step is to put numbers associated with these items and events. "So, how much do you spend on cars?"

"I don't know how much."

"Well, what about your last car? How much was that car? Is that the kind of car you like to drive?"

Again, it's a conversation. It's all inside the client. We just have to get it out and our process gets it out.

Most important is that it must be relevant and meaningful to The Better Life. We keep saying, "If this is what you're spending your money on does that support you in living The Better Life?" Because there's more to The Better Life than spending money, but trust me when it's cold outside it's nice to have a warm house and when it's hot outside it's nice to have an air-conditioned house. It's part of living The Better Life. The key here is to be engaged and to have fun in the process.

As you're reading this book, I want you to reflect and ask yourself the question, "What is important to me about money?"

Ask yourself the question, "What am I going to spend my money on?"

Ask the question, "How much do I want to spend?"

Ask the question, "How long do I really want to work?"

You want to ask yourself all these questions so you can get engaged with your life while you're reading this book. As we present to you this strategic solution, you've got to continuously keep in mind that this strategic solution has one goal and one goal only; that you and your partner live a Better Life.

The better definition I have of The Better Life, the greater probability I will have of achieving it. It is totally unique to me. Nobody else will have the same definition. There may be a lot of similarities, but there will be uniqueness to it and it's that Better Life, that engagement that gets you to take action, which gets you to make things happen. We really want you to sit and reflect upon this.

Once we have all the pieces together we add them up, but we add them up strategically not just numerically, because part of the awareness and part of the impact is not only knowing the individual numbers, but it's knowing the individual components and how they relate. We also relate your spending to your income. Through this book we are using The Case Study of a typical Middle Class Canadian as outlined in Appendix A. Over 25 years this couple, making $150,000 a year, will earn $3,750,000. In Canada they'll pay tax and that will leave about $2,760,000. If they're living on $60,000 a year that will eat up $1,500,000. That leaves them $1,260,000. With their existing debt and future commitments of $1,610,000 including interest, they'll quickly find that they cannot afford their life.

When we take you through this process, it helps identify the problem. What is important here is that you can relate to it because it's your life we are talking about. We will have reviewed your pay stub, which will include tax, CPP, EI, other deductions, etc. and we will identify what you're living on. Then we'll look at the commitments. These numbers will be your life and you'll be engaged with them. You'll realize you don't have enough money.

This is where our Baby Boomers find themselves.

When I say, "Adding things up strategically," I mean it's relevant to your life and you can connect with it. You say, "Yes, this is my life," and this is the way the numbers flow. I basically have a shortfall. Well, now I'm really interested in the solution to the problem because it's scoped out and it's relevant to you individually. Occasionally we find couples that are really living modestly to what their income is and they have a surplus and we deal with that in a different way, but most people will find their numbers show that if they continue the path they're on; they'll be where the Baby Boomers are today.

Susan: Which is having to work until they're 85?

Doug: That's right. They'll have personal debt in their mid-60s, which of course, is terrible to have.

Susan: How far out do you look for people?

Doug: We generally look from 15 to 25 years out. Further out than that it's difficult for people to relate to. If I'm sitting across from someone who's 35 years of age we will look out to age 60. We try to get them to think and live out their life at the meetings and then we put numbers associated with it. As I say the dollars flow from their life.

Susan: Essentially what you're doing is you're projecting out from today into their future. If they live their journey using the conventional method the majority find they are coming up short.

Doug: Yes, in other words, the problem my wife and I had in the late 70's is still the same problem today. It hasn't changed one bit. And in fact may even be worse.

Susan: We literally can't save that much, unless we're really talking about a huge reduction in lifestyle and I don't know anyone who wants to do that.

Doug: For us, it is The Better Life only when you can live the life you want in your working years and have the retirement you hoped and dreamed of. We want a solution that moves beyond what the conventional methods can deliver. Now there are some people where the hole is so deep that they have to work longer and have to save more. But because they came to us, it's a lot less than that conventional method.

This is not a new problem. When I was in my early 20's I identified this problem and most people told me, "Doug, it's not a problem. You're only 20 years of age. What do you know about life?" Well, I knew a lot about math, but not much about life. I knew it just wasn't going to work because the numbers didn't support it.

Susan: I love that you're saying you don't have to sacrifice today to have The Better Life. That's why I think a lot of people resist looking for solutions. They worry the answers to being happy when you're 70, is that you need to be unhappy when you're 30 to 60. They have to live a restricted life. So a lot of people think, "Well, I'll worry about that when I'm 70."

Doug: "In your working years live The Better Life and save so you can continue The Better Life in your retirement years." It's about having The Better Life all along the way.

The next step in this process is the partnership. It's the team that cares about you. That team is made up of your spouse, friends and professionals. There's a financing side. There's an investment side. There's a tax side. There's an insurance side. There's a legal side. The first thing to realize is that for those five professionals you need a coordinator of those pieces and for the middle-class Canadian there's nobody who's connecting financing, investment, tax, insurance and legal into a cohesive process to make it happen. These are the people you need on your team. The most important person on this team if it's a married person is their spouse. It's not that the others are less important. They just play a different role. But they are needed on your team. There is one other team member that's critical. This is a key aspect of what the GPS Process provides.

It is a massive job for an individual, on their own, to find all these relationships and to get them all to work together. Most people don't have the time, the resources, or the connections to make that happen.

If you're worth $5 million, people are lined up to offer you the team, but if you're a 35-year-old with debt nobody's interested in making this happen. Again, with the GPS Process, we make that happen.

When you partner with The GPS Process, our team implements the plan with you as an integral part of the process. In our process the client makes all the decisions and then they delegate implementation where it makes sense. For some things they're actively involved in it. For other things they can delegate to the team. There are going to be changes in the journey that you need to direct as well. I don't care how well you plan, it will not be the plan you live. It's important to put it on paper to be a guideline, but there will be changes. Some of those changes can include: lay-offs, timing of purchases, and higher cost of purchases.

Also, as part of the partnership, you meet with a Coach regularly, every six months. Between meetings, you have a Consultant that is available, when needed, if there are questions or implementations along the way. Think of the Coach at the regular meetings as your Chief Financial Officer and they're directing things with you. There's support needed along the way and our organization provides that support.

Then you need a model to pull this all together. A model that can calculate affordability! There are lots of models out there that are good adding machines, but they're not good at calculating affordability.

"Can I really afford my life?" They'll tell you what your net asset at the end is, but that is not enough. Again, as part of the process when people work with us, we've developed a customized model that can figure that out because the conventional model only goes so far.

Partnership is important because you need a team to support you. No different than a team in sports. No different than a team in business, but how many middle-class Canadians have a team supporting them? Most can't afford it and they say, "If I pay the team I have less money for my Better Life." Well, if that team adds value, then you have more money, so partnership is important. Also, partnership is part of celebration. When one of our clients hits a major milestone we celebrate. When they pay off their debt, we celebrate. You feel as if there's a group out there that cares about you. You can turn to them when there are changes and to make it happen.

Just think about it for a minute. If you work with an organization for 20 years and you're meeting them every six months that's 40 meetings. If you make a key decision at every one of those meetings, that's 40 key decisions. That will transform your life and each of those decisions is solely focused on your goals, solely focused on your Better Life. We made this strategic decision so that you can afford your Better Life and have The Better Life. Imagine making 40 critical decisions over time? That will change your life and then when you add acceleration through our technology, it becomes a WOW factor.

Susan: Agreed!

Doug: I encourage people who read the book to think about the team members they need. The team members even go beyond financial because this is also about your well-being.

Susan: It's about your whole life, isn't it?

Doug: It is and that life should be exciting, fulfilling and impactful. I don't know about you, Susan, but if I don't get up in the morning thinking I'm going to do something impactful and make a contribution, I might as well go back to bed.

Let's get into the strategies.

Here's the challenge.

You calculate your life. You include your income and your spending. You add in growth, inflation and interest and end up with a shortfall. How can you take exactly the same assumptions, don't put anything more in, don't change any other assumptions and get a better result? How do you realize The Better Life when the inputs are identical??

The GPS Process acts as an accelerator that transforms your life from unaffordable to affordable with no change in interest rates, market growth, or your input. In other words, everything is the same.

You add a strategic accelerator that moves you from shortfall to surplus. How's that possible?

That's where we come in with the GPS Process. Our solution doesn't require you to put any more money in, nor does it ask you to chase higher growth, nor will it require you to work longer, because these are not necessary. How is it possible to have all the same assumptions as the conventional way and you solve the problem? It sounds like magic. It sounds like it's not possible. Well, that's where you go from the horse and buggy to the car. In other words, understanding what else can change. First of all, you've got to have a mindset change. You have to believe that you're not working in a world of financial scarcity. You're working in the world of financial abundance.

When I took economics in first year at University it opened with saying, "Economics is the allocation of scarce resources." When I took economics, as my youngest daughter said, "That was 200 or 300 years ago, so things have changed a little." In reality most people still have the scarcity mindset not abundance. The first thing we have to do is we have to get people to at least entertain the idea that there's abundance out there and get rid of that scarcity mindset. You're just not tapped into it. It's really quite simple. We set up a process where you attract additional cash flow with your resources. It is not your cash flow that we're attracting, it is **additional** cash flow!

To start that process you must both harvest and plant at the same time. The key is to attract additional cash flow by investing while you're paying for the commitments so you both harvest and plant on your life journey. You do this with a safe and secure structure. You need to set a structure in between your life and the result. Everybody is using some sort of method or structure to pay for their life, whether they realize it or not. For most people it is very inefficient.

The first step in setting a structure up is to realize how you manage your cash flow for your day-to-day living is different than how you manage your cash flow for your personal debt, future commitments and savings. If I meet someone who says, "I'm putting so much to my day-to-day living and I'm putting so much to my debt." I'm going to say to them, "That debt payment is your gold mine." That is what we can multiply. We're not going to change your day-to-day living expenses. That's what we call "Life Flow." The balance is your "Contribution Flow" which for most people includes your other debt payments such as: car loan, a mortgage, or savings. We take the "Contribution Flow" and we transform that to a whole new level of impact.

Let me give you an example with a mortgage. Someone is presently making a mortgage payment that will pay it off in 14 years. With an interest rate of 5% on a $200,000 mortgage, that would cost them about $283,000 in total. Using our GPS Process, with no change in your input, we can change your amortization from 14 to 9 years.

What happens if you continue to make the same mortgage payment from years 10 to 14 as planned? At the end of it you have an additional cash flow of $289,000. In other words, the GPS Process allows you to not only recover the interest you paid on the mortgage, but recover the principal and have some money left over.

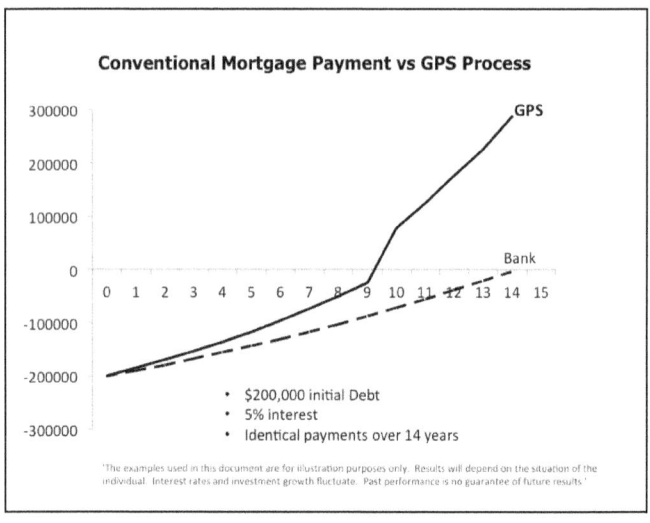

I always smile when the banks say; "We can lower your interest rate by a 10th or a quarter percent."

I say; "Mr. Banker, I want to get 0% interest from you and I want you to pay for all my debt."

They look at me like I'm nuts and say, "That's not possible."

I like to hear that because it reminds me that they're not competitors to the GPS Process.

The GPS Process can reduce the cost of your mortgage significantly. Just imagine if you:

applied that same concept to cars,

applied that concept to home improvements

or you applied that concept to your kids' education,

or you applied that concept to your kids' weddings,

or you applied that concept to renovating your kitchen?

You have to start with a financial structure. You need a structure in place because one of the pillars to this process is a word that causes fear in the financial services world. It is called "leveraging." Leveraging is when you borrow money to invest. This is what we call "Smart Debt" because "Smart Debt" attracts cash flow. It has been around for a long time and is used regularly and successfully by businesses and wealthy people.

The GPS Process allows you to be "smart" and leverage. This will allow you to afford your life. Most people who leverage do it without a structure and do it unsafely. If you're going to do this strategy then you have to do it within a structure, because that ensures the necessary safety and security. I say to people, "You don't move from the horse and buggy to the car, unless the car has breaks and seat belts in it." In other words, there are all these safety measures you put in place to go from traveling at 30 to 100 kilometers an hour. I wouldn't drive a Model T at 100 kilometers an hour, but most people leverage with a Model T at that speed and they fail.

Let's say someone presently has a mortgage of $200,000 and over time we re-plant that money. You need a structure which allows you to do both, allows you to both pay for the commitments and do the investing. Realistically, the dollar happens twice.

What is "smart", safe and secure leveraging? Firstly, you must have a long-term view on the investment. You must fully understand your cash flow. In other words, be confident you can make the monthly payment to the mortgage, which you're already doing. You must use conservative equity investing. Many people leverage and then they go out and buy highly volatile stocks. What we are talking about here is conservative.

You must set up, manage and document your structure because with the Canadian tax rules, when you borrow money to invest, the interest is tax deductible. But, when you borrow money for consumption (to buy a car) the interest is not tax deductible. The audit trail is critical and that's part of having the GPS Team in place. One of the nice things about Smart Debt is you take the tax savings and use it to pay off the personal debt. Smart Debt pays your personal debt off faster.

Also, Smart Debt takes you beyond the math of the amortization table. It takes you into math of quantum mechanics. I'm not going to go into that in detail in this book but it's a whole, new level of math. When people do leveraging they must do it with a structure of safety and security. That's one of the things we specialize in. We work with people to set up "smart" structures. We have 400 clients who we've been doing this with for over 30 years. We've gone through up markets and down markets. Our clients have always succeeded. We must know something that makes it work and the key is we set up structures with Smart Debt.

The question becomes, "Do you want to follow the conventional view that may require you to get 20% growth to accomplish your objectives or do you want to follow our view which requires you to get 6% growth using "Smart" Debt?" I would say needing over 20% growth is a much higher risk strategy than only needing 6%." That's where you've got to have the attitude change. We work with clients to grow their comfort zone. Most middle-class Canadians use leveraging in a way that exposes them to risk, not reducing risk. Our GPS Process is specifically about reducing that risk.

Susan: Doug, can you share a specific example of how middle-class Canadians are using leverage and exposing themselves to too much risk?

Doug: Oh yes. Someone will go out and borrow $100,000 when the market's high. They got a hot tip on the market. It's going to keep going up. They borrow $100,000, and then go buy something of high risk hoping for a big payday. They go buy a resource stock. They go buy a penny stock. They say, "All I can lose is a penny." Well, you can lose everything. They usually buy at a peak because everybody else is buying and they usually buy a high risk investment hoping to hit it big. Someone will tell them, "You can use the growth in the investments to pay the interest on the loan." It's a recipe for disaster. What happens if there's no growth? You've got to make sure you understand your cash flow and they expect a quick rate of return so when it goes down they sell low because they can't make the payment. I see it all the time.

One of the exciting parts of the GPS Process is that it gives you The Better Life. Another exciting part of the process is that it creates consistent Cash Flow. Because of this you don't need 15%++ return on your equities to create The Affordable Life. With The GPS Process you just need 6% to 8%. "Smart" Debt reduces the risk. People if left to their own devices, buy at a peak, buy too risky of a stock, don't understand their cash flow and don't have the right set of expectations going in. When the Stock Market goes down, it's a Strategic buying opportunity, not a reactionary selling situation.

The next thing that will transform a person's life is inflation. People's salaries go up. It will go up over the next 25 years. For most people inflation is a liability. In other words, things cost more. At the same time people forget there's inflation on their income and most people aren't aware how much their incomes have gone up. We're talking about middle-class Canadians who have a very good chance of their income going up.

If your income goes up by 3% you need to intentionally allocate a portion of that increase to Life Flow and a portion to Contribution Flow. If a person just does that it will transform their life. The problem is that these increases are so small, especially when you divide them over 26 pays. As well, many increases happen in January, which is the same time that your CPP and EI deductions start again. Many people actually have less cash flow in January than in

December, even with a salary increase. But because of CPP and EI starting again they say, "Well, I don't really get an increase until later on."

If you intentionally allocate out your increases between your Life Flow (day-to-day living) and your Contribution Flow (which is your personal debt, future commitments and savings), then what happens is every year you increase your debt payment by the proportional amount. If your debt payment is $30,000 a year and you get an inflation increase of 3% then an extra $900 per year would go to your debt payment. If it happens over 26 pays that's about $35 per pay, the difference is small. That's like going out for a very inexpensive Friday night dinner. It just gets lost in the shuffle.

If you take those little differences and you add them up over the years and you have a structure to be intentional, then all of a sudden it builds at an accelerated pace. That's why you need a structure because that structure allows you to capture those accelerated inflationary increases. There's a wide range of excuses along the way that prevent you from doing that. Again, that's why you need your goals. That's why you need the partnership so you can identify that cash flow. Those little slivers that add up over time make the difference. In the Case Study used in this book, those slivers make a $632,000 difference over 25 years.

On the flip side if you keep adding those inflationary increases to your life flow, in reality every year little by little, it's costing you more and more to live in real terms, which means you need a bigger asset base at the end, which means you've got more debt, etc.

Inflation can work for you and against you and for most people inflation works against you. This is what happened to most Baby Boomers. With our process it works for you.

To give you some idea of the scope, let's go back to the mortgage example (see page 33 for Mortgage Example) where we move from 14 years to 9 years with $289,000 at the end. If you add inflation recovery to that model, it moves the amortization to 7 years and increases the number at the end to $425,000. You're going to say, "Inflation makes that much of a difference?" It's the old compounding scenario, but at an accelerated level.

If you understand your living expenses, if you have a structure to flow things through, a structure that uses "Smart Debt" and if you optimize inflation, for most people that is enough to get you over the hump, to fill the gap and you don't need to earn more money. You don't need to get more growth and you don't need to work longer. In essence, as ironic as this may sound, we can tell you how much "Smart Debt" you need to afford your life. This pays your house off faster, pays your commitments off faster and then we work with the reality of your salary increases as you go through your life journey.

The last piece, which is very important, is income tax. It is critical that the middle-class Canadian use income tax planning beyond just contributing to RRSPs. It's not that those aren't important, but they are limited as to how much you can do. Also, you may not have the cash flow to make the contributions. When you save income tax using the GPS Process, you have more cash flow. When you invest using the GPS

Process, you have more investment growth. Not because of a higher rate of return, but because you're investing more earlier rather than less later. Because of this, you have a bigger asset base at the end of the process. When you retire, you want to protect your asset base by taking the cash out in the most tax-efficient way. Tax planning plays a very important role. In the working years you have the additional cash flow to build your asset base, and maybe more importantly, in the retirement years you are paying less in taxes when receiving income.

Let me give you an example. If someone needs to top up their cash flow above their pension income by $40,000 a year, if that person's tax rate is 30%, they need to withdraw $57,000 to net $40,000. If you can organize it so that the person's effective tax rate is 5%, then they will only have to withdraw $42,000 to net $40,000. You need a much smaller asset base to replace $42,000 than $57,000. Tax planning is an accelerator in the form of reducing your taxes so you have more cash flow, but it's also an accelerator in the form of needing a smaller asset base to afford your life. If you don't do tax planning combined with inflation and with "Smart Debt", it's like having a three-legged stool trying to balance with only two legs. Tax planning is critical in this process to create wealth and to take it out in the tax-efficient way. Again, we look at all scenarios.

Susan: This is some pretty phenomenal information you are sharing.

Doug: It works. The math and cash flow can't be denied.

Susan: In the earlier example where you showed the couple who are 35 making $150,000 a year and looking out to age 60, how big of a gap did they have?

Doug: Actually it's quite staggering. As modest as the life is that the example portrays, in the end, there is over a million-dollar gap between the life they want and the life they can afford. Using conventional methods they would not be able to afford the life that they desire. They would be forced to work longer and live on less along the way. Conversely, the GPS Process eliminates the million-dollar gap. They can maintain their lifestyle and pay for the commitments that they have identified. The GPS Process is the only way I know for them to live their Better Life. The traditional method will not help them live better.

Susan: Wow. That's quite a difference.

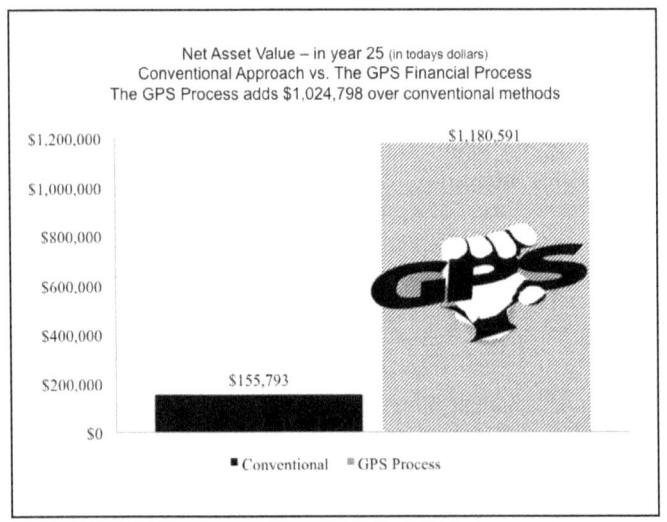

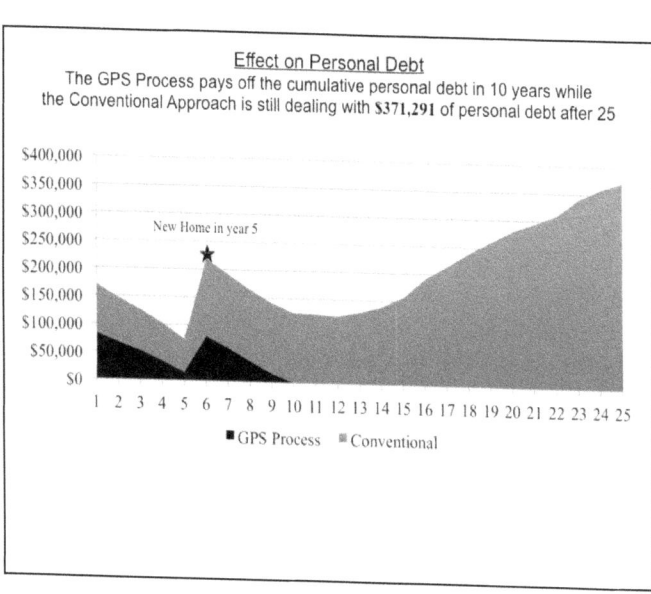

Chapter 5 – Next Steps

The GPS Process is as much about Leadership and Support as it is about building a financial structure, applying the math and understanding the cash flow. Real Financial Planning, Financial Leadership is a lifetime process. It's not a one-time event. We offer to the average Canadian family the services and the connections that previously were exclusively for the wealthiest of individuals. We found a better way to do things so that we could afford our life. We took a look at the existing system, came to the conclusion that it's broken and we fixed it. We learned that we couldn't fix it within the existing box. The horse and buggy were not going to do it for us. We had to move to a whole new box. We learned there is a better way. We kept the pieces that made sense. For example, we didn't get rid of the mortgage amortization table. We just use it better.

We believe that everyone is doing the best they can, the best they know. But we absolutely believe that there is a better way for the middle class to do things than the Financial Industry is offering. There is a famous quote from Maya Angelou that sums it up best:

"Do the best you can until you know better.

Then when you know better, do better."

Do you want The Better Life? Do you want to know that you can afford that life, and most likely afford more? How would you live if you knew that your life was paid for?

How does this sound?

Your life,

> Your Better Life,

>> is paid,

>>> PAID in FULL!

Susan: I want to thank you Doug. What you've done here is taken a very complex problem most people do not fully understand and given us a solution for it.

Doug: We took the time to figure out the system is broken and provided you with a different, better system, The GPS Process.

Thank you, Susan, for hosting this.

Appendix A

A Case Study

A couple age 35 with 2 children

A Combined Gross Income of $150K with a Net Income of $110.4K. Deductions include Income Tax, CPP, EI and other deductions.

Day to Day Living Expenses (Life Flow) are $60K annually. This does not include any debt payments and savings (Contribution Flow).

They own a House with a Market Value of $350K.

Their total Personal debt is $200K.

Investments include:
- RRSP $50K
- RESP $20K
- Total $70K

Plan period – Years 2015 to 2039 – 25 years.

Future Commitments without inflation include:
1. Car #1 - $35K replacing every 6 years starting Year 2016.
2. Car #2 - $25K replacing every 6 years starting Year 2017.
3. Home Upgrade of $150K in Year 2020
4. Annual Home Improvements from Years 2029 to 2039 - $4K per year

5. 2 Children:
    a. Post Secondary - $20K per year for 4 years.
    b. Wedding- $15K each.
6. Total of above with Inflation is $889K.

Economic indicators
1. Inflation – 3%.
2. Financing – 6%.
3. Investment Growth - 6%.

Government pension plans included as eligible.

Total cost of Commitments:
1. Existing Personal Debt $ 200K
2. Future Commitments $ 889K
3. Interest $ 521K
4. Total $1,610K

Allocation of Gross Income for 25 years:
1. Annual Gross Income of $150K $3,750K
2. Income tax and Other Deductions $ 990K
3. Net Income $2,760K
4. Life Flow - $60K annually $1,500K
5. Total Commitments from above $1,610K
6. Total Life Flow and Commitments $3,110K
7. Shortfall $ 350K

About the Author

After pursuing his love of accounting, finance and economics at University, Doug went to work for a Canadian Fortune 500 Company. During this period he spent his spare time helping others with their budgeting and financial planning.

Doug realized very quickly that the financial industry was not focused on the middle class and did not have solutions for their biggest financial issues. Doug developed what is arguably the first Financial Planning Process for the middle class in Canada. With the solution now proven and the demand for his solution growing, it was time to help others full time. With the help and support of his wife Shirley, Triple Win Inc. became a reality.

Thirty years later, The GPS Process has impacted more than 500 clients!

Doug's Better Life includes Family, Math, Charity, Reading, Cycling for health and Tennis for entertainment.

What does your Better Life include?